Pierre Boucher, Edward Louis Montizambert

Canada in the seventeenth Century

Pierre Boucher, Edward Louis Montizambert

Canada in the seventeenth Century

ISBN/EAN: 9783337186524

Printed in Europe, USA, Canada, Australia, Japan

Cover: Foto ©ninafisch / pixelio.de

More available books at **www.hansebooks.com**

CANADA

IN THE

SEVENTEENTH CENTURY.

FROM THE FRENCH OF PIERRE BOUCHER.

BY

EDWARD LOUIS MONTIZAMBERT.

MONTREAL:

PRINTED BY GEORGE E. DESBARATS & CO.

1883

TRANSLATOR'S PREFACE.

So many persons who do not understand French, now take an interest in the early state of this part of Canada, that the time seems to me to have come for an English version of the following work to meet with acceptance.

Its author was a brave and hardy Norman, who quitted the old world for the new at an early age, and both for one that is better than either at a very advanced one. Born in France about 1620, he came to Quebec, with his father, Gaspard Boucher, in 1635, and died at Boucherville, near Montreal, in 1717*—having served his King and country zealously and well, in Canada, for many years, from 1639.

For such his services in general, and for his gallant and successful defence of the fort at Three Rivers against Indians, in August 1653 in particular, he was handsomely rewarded by the former, and he has ever been held in grateful remembrance by the latter.

He was Governor of the settlement at Three Rivers, from July 1653 to July 1658, and from November 1662 to some time between September 166⅞ and April 1668.

Charlevoix writes of him as follows:

" By the last vessels that sailed from Quebec, † this
" general, Baron d'Avaugour, and all the persons in
" office in the country, had written strongly to the Court,
" to implore the King to take under his protection a
" colony which was utterly abandoned and reduced to
" the last extremity."

---

* The entry in the register of the Parish Church, recording his burial under his own pew, in it sets forth that he was aged about ninety seven, (*âgé d'environ nonante sept ans.*)

† 22nd October, 1661,—E. L. M.

" They had committed their memorials to the Sieur
" Boucher, who commanded at Three Rivers ; and much
" was hoped from the zeal of that officer, who was better
" acquainted with Canada than any other, and whose
" virtues fitted him in the highest degree to obtain a
" favourable hearing from the Prince."

" He was indeed very well received by His Majesty,
" who manifested great surprise on learning that so fine
" a country had met with such neglect."

In an article in the *Rose-Belford Canadian Monthly
Magasine*, for November 1880, Mr. William Kingsford
very justly says of him : " That he was the first Canadian
" ennobled by Louis XIV., * is a trifling matter compared
" to the reputation he has left of honesty, ability, courage
" and worth."

His fame being so great, and his memory being so highly
respected in his own part of Canada, I am proud to be able
to trace my descent from him. My father's father, who was
allowed † to take the *surnom* of de Montizambert, was a
son of one of his sons, Jean Baptiste Boucher de Niverville.

I shall therefore feel myself to be sufficiently compen-
sated for whatever this translation may have cost me,
in any way, by the consciousness of having done what I
could towards making more of my English-speaking
fellow-countrymen acquainted with our author, through
his unpretending little descriptive sketch of the Canada,
in whose prosperity and advancement he took so deep
and so effectual an interest, more than two centuries ago.

E. L. MONTIZAMBERT.

QUEBEC, 8 April, 1881.

* In 1661, before his mission to France.
† In the official muster-roll of a French regiment, dated and signed at la
Rochelle, 18th August, 1661, his name is entered among those of the officers
remaining in Canada as de Niverville de Montizambert.

TRUE AND GENUINE DESCRIPTION

OF

NEW FRANCE,

COMMONLY CALLED CANADA,

AND OF THE MANNERS AND CUSTOMS AND PRODUCTIONS OF THAT COUNTRY.

BY

PIERRE BOUCHER.

P ARIS:
FLORENTIN LAMBERT.

1664

The author of this little work is not the Jesuit Father Pierre Boucher, as the Abbé Lenglet du Fresnoy supposed, but the Sieur Pierre Boucher, Governor of Three Rivers, one of the first settlers of New France, where, imitating the simplicity and piety of the patriarchs, he participated in the blessings which God bestowed upon them, having seen his numerous and flourishing posterity to the fifth generation. He was deputed to the Court to represent the spiritual and temporal wants of the colony ; and during this voyage to Europe he printed the little relation in question, which contains only a quite superficial but very faithful account of Canada.—*Shea's Charlevoix*. Vol. 1, p. 80.

DEDICATION.

To Monseigneur Colbert, Counsellor of the King in His Royal Council, Intendant of Finance, and Superintendent of His Majesty's Buildings, Baron Seignelay, &c.,

My Lord,

Having written a succinct, but correct account and natural history of New France, which is watered by the great river Saint Lawrence and its tributary lakes and rivers, I deem this dedication of the work to be due to you, God having given you a singular love of this country, which will no doubt go on increasing when you shall have been more fully informed of the fertility and beauty of all these regions.

All those who know you agree in thinking that the surest way to interest you in any subject, is to show you that the King's glory and the interests of France are concerned in connection with it, and that when that has been done, one may count upon your exertions and influence being put forth in regard to it, with the happiest results.

Such being the case, I have thought, my Lord, that this statement might contribute in some degree to the increase of the inclination you have already. to cause this New France of ours to prosper, and to make a new world of it, when you learn from the contents, written in my simple and artless style, that it really is worth peopling, and that it could easily receive the overflowings of the population of Old France, which is so rich in men and women, that foreign kingdoms and their colonies are being peopled with them from day to day.

Would it not be better that the King should keep his subjects for himself, by causing them to pass over into New France, and that the French name should become equally renowned in both worlds, in America and in Europe.

I should have reason to fear that this work would not be well received by those who look for graces of style in the use of our language, if I did not remember that having had the honour, last year, to speak to His Majesty, and to answer several questions which he put to me respecting New France, my simple and artless answers were so far from seeming to be distasteful to him, that, on the contrary, he had the goodness to express gratification with them.

I have thought, my Lord, that you would not have less kindness towards me, and that, accepting this little present, which I offer to you with all my heart, you will give your patronage to it, and permit me to subscribe myself,

My Lord,

Your very humble and very obedient servant,

PIERRE BOUCHER.

From the town of Three Rivers, in New France, the 8th of October, 1663.

PREFACE.

You are to know, my dear readers, that I have two reasons for writing this little treatise. The first is, that I was invited by many respectable people, whom I had the honour to converse with, while I was in France, and who took great pleasure in hearing about this country, and in being disabused of the unfavourable opinions they had entertained of it in some respects, to send them some account of this New France, that is to say, of what the country is like and of what is to be found in it, in order that they might make it known to their friends. The number of those who asked me to do so being great, it would not have been without difficulty that I could have complied with their requests, and therefore, I resolved to have this description printed, and to beg of them to have recourse to it.

The second reason is, that having become aware of His Majesty's affection for his New France, and of his resolution to destroy our enemies, the Iroquois, and to cause this country to be peopled, I thought that I should oblige many persons who might have a mind to come here, or to send some of their relations here, by making the country known to them before they came.

I had long had a thought of this kind in my mind, and I always hoped that some one would take a pen in hand for the above purpose ; but seeing that no one made it his duty to do so, I resolved to write this description, while waiting for some one else to write one in more elegant language, because, for my part, I have contented myself with merely writing to you of facts as they are,

2

without seeking for fine language, to do it in,; telling you
the truth indeed, but telling it as simply and as briefly as
possible, and omitting everything that I thought would
be superfluous and such things as would only have served
to embellish the treatise.

I shall tell you hardly any thing that has not been told
already and that you cannot find in the Reverend Jesuit
Fathers' narratives *(Relations)* or in Monsieur de Cham-
plain's travels ; but as what I have set down here has not
been collected into one book before, and as all the
Narratives would have to be read in order to find it all,
this will be a help for you, and above all for those who
have no other object than to learn what sort of a country
New France is, and who do not trouble themselves about
what has happened or about what is happening here.
That is the reason why I shall not speak of events,
although something happened here this year that was
very extraordinary, and such as I had never seen the
like of during the thirty years or so that I have been in
this country ; and that was an earthquake, the shocks of
which were felt repeatedly during seven months. particularly about Tadousac, where it made itself felt very much.
Some wonderful commotions of the earth took place there.
We had some shocks at Three Rivers in the beginning.
and they extended even to Montreal. But the best thing
of all in connection with all these dreadful overturnings
and concussions was, that God so kept us as that not a
single person suffered the slightest inconvenience from
them. I shall not say any thing more about this earthquake ; the Reverend Jesuit Fathers, in their Narratives,
have described it and all the effects it produced much
better than I could, and in a way to give you much more
pleasure in reading of it than I could.

You will see in the following pages what are the
temporal advantages to be enjoyed in this country; I
mean advantages as concerns the things of this world.
In spiritual matters nothing better than we have could be
wished for. We have a Bishop whose zeal and virtue are
such that I could not say enough of them. He is all
things to all men. He makes himself poor to make the
poor rich ; and he resembles the Bishops of the primitive
Church. He is assisted by several secular priests, persons
of great merit, for he cannot put up with any who are
not. The Jesuit Fathers second his designs, labouring
indefatigably with their usual zeal, for the salvation of
the French and of the Indians.

In one word, good people may live here very con-
tentedly ; but not bad people, because they are two closely
looked after here ; therefore, I do not advise any such
to come, because they might be expelled from the country,
or at the least compelled to leave it, as many have done
already ; and it is precisely those who loudly decry the
country, not having found in it what they expected.

I have no doubt that those persons, who were the
scum of New France, when they hear this description of
mine read, will say that I have told more than the truth ;
and perhaps other persons also will say the same thing,
not through malice, but through ignorance ; but I assure
you, my dear readers, that I have seen the greater part
of all that I speak of, and that I have learned the rest
from very trustworthy persons.

I know very well that you will find other faults, and
even many in the very order of narration ; but I think
you will forgive me for them very willingly when you
consider that composition is not in my line, and moreover,
that I have only written this short account of New

France, in order to oblige several persons, in anticipation of a more exact one being written by some more able pen than mine, and in a more elegant style. It is partly for this reason that I have omitted a number of things worthy of the attention of a curious reader, and have sought only to be as brief as possible, and still to make known what it was absolutely necessary to have known.

NATURAL HISTORY OF CANADA

CHAPTER I.

OF NEW FRANCE IN GENERAL.

Speaking of New France as a whole, I may say that it is a good country, and one that contains in itself a good portion of all that can be wished for. The soil is very good, it produces wonderfully well, and is not ungrateful; we have had experience of that. The country is covered with dense and very fine forests, that are stocked with numbers of animals of various kinds; and what is of still greater consequence, is that those forests are intersected by large and small rivers of very good water, and have in them numbers of springs and fountains : besides which there are large and small lakes, bordered as well as the rivers by fine large prairies which produce as good grasses as there are in France. In these lakes and rivers there are great numbers of fish of all kinds, very good and very dainty; water fowl are also to be met with in great numbers on these lakes and rivers; the country is a very healthy one; animals brought from France thrive very well in it; one sees here many fine plants that are not to be found in France; there are few plants here that are injurious to man, and, on the other hand, there are many simples here the effects of which are wonderfully good. There are also few noxious animals here. Salt springs have been found, from which very good salt can be got, and also mineral springs. There is one of the latter in the Iroquois country which gives out a greasy water that is like oil, and is used in many cases instead of oil. There are also beds of several ores here, it is said : what I am certain of, is that there are some of iron and some of copper in several places ; divers trustworthy persons have assured me that there is a very rich one of lead, not very far from us ; but as it is near a path our enemies frequent, no one has yet ventured to go and explore it. The climate is different in different places ; but I may say of it in general that in the coldest place here winter is a more cheerful season than it is in France. I will give fuller information on this head when I treat of e ch thing in particular, as I hope to do for the satisfaction of the reader.

New France is a very large country. It is divided in two by a great river, called the Saint Lawrence, the mouth of which begins at Gaspé, and is fifty leagues wide ; as for the length of the river, we only know that it takes its rise in Lake Huron, otherwise called the fresh water sea, which is considered to be about three hundred leagues in circumference, and that from Gaspé to the said lake is about five hundred leagues, following the windings of the river.

Into this lake or fresh water sea another lake called Superior discharges itself, which is hardly second to it in any respect, according to the report of it that has been made to us by the Indians of that country, and also by Frenchmen lately come from thence.

All that great country remains unknown to us, by reason of the war with the Iroquois, which prevents us from exploring it, as it is desirable we should.

It is true that there is something dreadful in the aspect of the approaches to this country called New France ;

for the sight of the Island of Newfoundland, on which is Placentia, of the Saint Pierre Islands, of Cape Ray, of St. Paul's Island, and of the mainland at the entrance of the Gulf, inspires dismay and an inclination to keep away from the country rather than a desire to come and live in it ; wherefore I am not surprised that this country was so long without becoming inhabited. All things considered, I think all that it lacks is inhabitants. That is why I have felt impelled to write this little treatise, for the purpose of giving correct information to all who may have any inclination for New France, and any desire to come and live here ; and to do away with the bad opinion that the common people have of it to such an extent, that we are very improperly threatened with having all the scapegraces sent here by way of punishment ; where as I can assure you that on the contrary, there are few of those who have come here who have any intention to return to France, unless called there by affairs of great importance ; and I tell you candidly that during my stay in Paris and elsewhere, last year, I met with many persons in easy circumstances who had formerly been inhabitants of Canada, and had left it on account of the war, who assured me that they were full of impatience to return to it ; so true is it that New France has attractions for those who know how to appreciate its delights.

In order to make the rest of this treatise more intelligible to you, I will tell you the distances between the different inhabited places and places that are remarkable for their harbours, or for other things.

I shall not say any thing about the entrance of the Gulf, which I have mentioned above as being a part of the country not worth writing about. I shall only say that

from Percée Island to Gaspé, is seven leagues; from
Gaspé to Tadousac, twenty four leagues; from Tadousac
to Quebec, thirty leagues; from Quebec to Three-Rivers,
thirty leagues; from Three-Rivers to Montreal, thirty
leagues; from Three-Rivers to the place of the lower
Iroquois, called Anieronnons, who live near New Holland,
is about eighty leagues; from Montreal to the place of
the middle Iroquois, called Onnontagueronnons, is likewise about eighty leagues; from Montreal to the country
where the Hurons formerly lived, is two hundred leagues.

All this great river and these great lakes are full of
beautiful islands, of all sizes. The great river runs from
west to east. The water in it is salt as far up as Cape
Tourmente, which is seven leagues below Quebec, and
the distance from Quebec to the great banks of Newfoundland, where people go to fish for cod, is computed
to be three hundred leagues.

In the neighbourhood of *Percée* Island, numbers of
very good oysters are found. There is also in that
quarter, a hill containing coal; and likewise, a little on
this side of it, a plaster quarry

It only remains for me to tell you the bearings of our
settlements, to make all that follows more intelligible.
Know then that Gaspé is in forty-nine degrees ten
minutes north latitude; Tadousac in forty-eight degrees
and a third; Quebec in forty-six degrees and three
fourths; Three-Rivers in forty-six degrees; Montreal in
forty-five degrees; the place of the middle Iroquois,
called Onnontagueronnons, where we had a settlement
formerly, in forty two degrees and a quarter.

CHAPTER II.

As I shall often have occasion to speak of Quebec, which is the principal settlement we have in New France, and the first place therein that was inhabited by Frenchmen, I think it proper that I should begin by giving a rough description of it for the benefit of my readers.

Quebec, then, is the principal settlement, in which the Governor-General of the whole country resides. It has a good fort and a good garrison, as well as a fine church, which serves as a Parish Church, and is as it were the Cathedral of the whole country. Divine Service is performed in this Church, with the same ceremonies as in the best parish Churches in France. It is also in this place that the Bishop resides. There is a Jesuit College here, and a Convent of Ursuline Nuns, who teach all the little girls, which does a great deal of good to the country, as well as the Jesuits' college, for the instruction, of all the youth of this rising Colony. There is likewise a Convent of Nuns with a Hospital *(Hospitalières)* to the great relief of the sick poor. It is a pity they have not a larger income.

Quebec is situated on the bank of the great river Saint Lawrence, which is about a short league wide at this place, where it flows between high banks. The fort, the Churches, the convents and the finest houses are built on the height; but many dwellings and warehouses are built at the foot of the hill, on the shore of the great river, for the sake of being near the ships which come

3

thus far, it being supposed that they could not go further without risk.

One league below Quebec, the river is divided in two by a beautiful island, called the Island of Orleans, which is about eighteen leagues in circumference, and on which there are several settlers : the land there is very good, and there are many prairies along the shores.

Quebec is built on rocky ground, and, in excavating for cellars, one gets stone to build with ; but this stone is not very good, and mortar does not stick to it; it is a kind of black marble ; but a league from there both up and down the river side, perfectly good stone that dresses well is to be found. At Quebec, there is lime stone, and clay for making bricks, tiles for paving or roofing, and other like things ; four or five hundred paces below the fort, the land is intersected by a beautiful river called the river Saint Charles, which is nearly a league broad at high tide, where it discharges itself into the great river ; but at low tide, the beach there is almost quite dry ; and that is a great convenience for the taking of fish, which affords a good supply of fresh provisions for the inhabitants of the place, particularly in the spring when an infinite number of shad are caught there.) Below the mouth of this river, the country becomes level. and is settled as much as seven leagues down. The tides are perfectly regular there ; they ebb for seven hours and flow for five hours, and are three quarters of an hour later each day.

Quebec is on the north side of the river, and the settlement extends some distance back, where the land is good. It extends also for three leagues up the river ; but the land there, is not so good ; and on the south shore also, the soil, although good, is a little less promising.

In all these quarters there is an abundance of fish of all sorts such as sturgeon, salmon, catfish, bar, shad, and many others; but I must not omit to mention the eel fishing which takes place in the autumn, and yields with an abundance incredible to all who have not witnessed it. There is a man who has taken more than fifty thousand for his own share. They are long and thick, and taste very well, much better than those in France; they are salted to keep the year round, which they do perfectly well, and they are very good food for working people.

Game is not so plenty now, within ten or twelve leagues of Quebec, as it used to be. All that remain are wild pigeons, which are to be found here in abundance every summer; some are killed even in the gardens in Quebec and in the other settlements; they stay only for four months during the summer season.

All sorts of seeds are sown in the fields, as well as in the gardens, and all come up very well, as I shall mention further on, notwithstanding the length of the winters.

Having mentioned the winters, I shall say a few words of the seasons. Properly speaking, there are only two to be reckoned here, for we pass suddenly from great cold to great heat, and from great heat to great cold; therefore, we speak only of Winter and Summer. Winter begins immediately after All Saints Day; that is to say, frosts begin then, and some time after that comes the snow, which lies on the ground until about the fifteenth of April, in ordinary years; for it melts sooner than that in some years, and later than that in others; but usually it is about the sixteenth that the ground becomes free from snow, and in a state to put forth plants and to be ploughed.

From the beginning of May, the heat is very great, and one would not think that one was coming out of a severe winter. The consequence is, that vegetation advances very rapidly, and that one sees the earth decked with green in less than no time; and indeed, it is wonderful to see that the grain which is sown in the latter part of April, and even from that to the twentieth of May, is harvested in the month of September, and is then very fine and good; and other things advance, in proportion, for we see that white headed cabbages, the seeds of which are sown here in the beginning of May, and which are transplanted about the twentieth, or from that to the twenty-fourth of June, are got in at the end of October, when they have heads that weigh from fifteen to sixteen pounds.

As for the winter season, although it lasts five months, during which the ground is covered with snow, and the cold is rather severe, still it is not disagreeable; the cold is exhilarating, and on most days the weather is calm and fine, and one does not find oneself at all inconvenienced by the cold. We go all about on the snow, by the aid of certain foot gear, made by the Indians, which we call snow-shoes, and which are very convenient. In truth the snow is less troublesome here than the mud is in France.

The seasons are not of the same duration in all parts of the country. In Three Rivers, there is nearly a month less of winter than there is in Quebec; in Montreal, about six weeks; and in the Iroquois country, there is only about one month of winter.

Quebec, although less favourably situated, as to climate, and as to its aspect, which is not a pleasant one, still has very great advantages in the number of its inhabitants, and in the fact of its being the stopping place of the ships that come from France.

Tadousac is the place where the ships touched formerly, and where their cargoes were discharged. before it was thought safe to bring them up as far as Quebec ; all that it has to recommend it is a fine almost land-locked bay, in which ships are well sheltered. the bay being deep and the anchorage good.

There is a beautiful river, called the Saguenay, which flows into and through the bay ; a chapel and a warehouse have been built at this place, also a small fort, on account of some Indians passing the summer there ; but no person has settled there, the country not being favourable for settlement, either on the score of soil, or on that of climate, although the fishing there is very good.

(But let me say a word about the settlement at Three Rivers.) The country around it is very good to look at ; a level country, not a hilly one, with very fine forests ; the land is intersected by several rivers and lakes, all of which have fine prairies along their shores, so that there are numbers of animals, particularly moose, cariboo and beavers, and a very great abundance of feathered game, and fish.

(The soil on the farms on which clearings have been begun is sandy, but still it produces wonderfully well, the sand being rich on the top. Houses have been built on the north side only.)

There are as it were two settlements here, separated from each other by a wide river which flows from the interior of the country, on the north side of the St. Lawrence, and is called the Three Rivers, because, being divided by islands, it forms as it were three rivers at this place.

Montreal, which is the last of our French settlements, lies further inland. It is situated on a fine large island, called the Island of Montreal. The land there is very good ; the soil is dark and full of stones, and in it grain yields abundantly ; every thing grows very well in it, but specially melons and onions ; fishing and shooting are very good there ; all the surrounding country is very fine, and the further up one goes towards where the Iroquois live, the more inviting it is. The land is level, with forests of large and uncommonly tall trees, and what shows the goodness of the soil is, that the woods are clear and not incumbered with undergrowth. It would be a very suitable country in which to hunt the deer that are there in abundance, if there were settlers in it who had horses for the purpose, and the Iroquois had been humbled a little, or, to speak more correctly, subdued. Most of the trees are oaks.

But let us not tarry so long on the way, and let us come at once to the great lake of the Iroquois, after having passed through more than two hundred islands that lie in the entrance to it, of which two thirds are only prairies, and the other third are conical rocks.

Let us not even pause to dwell upon the great number of animals that are met with on the right and left banks of the river and on the islands, animals of which there are often more than five hundred in one herd.

This country of the Iroquois, of which I desire to speak, and which is on the bank of our great river, since that flows through their great lake, is a very good and pleasant country. The land in it is very good, if not the best that can be met with, so far as one can judge from the trees. Hardly any groves of fir are to be met with there, but on the contrary only fine forests

of oak, chestnut, walnut, beech, lime, mulberry, and·
numbers of other fine trees, which we are not acquainted
with in these parts, so that I do not know their names.
Fruit trees are more abundant there also : and so are
deer and other game. There are also several springs of
salt water there, from which good salt is made. The
extent of prairie land there is wonderful ; and the four
seasons are the same as in France, except that the
winter is not so long. Fish are also very abundant there,
especially salmon, sturgeon, catfish, and eels, of which
there are prodigious quantities. All those great countries
there are the same.

I shall not speak of the country of the Hurons,
because it has been abandoned by the French as well
as by those Indians, who have been obliged to leave
it on account of the Iroquois. That country is a very
fine and good one, almost all cleared, as France is,
situated on the shores of a great lake which is three
hundred leagues in circumference, and is full of islands
of all sorts of sizes and shapes, with fine timber, good
land, abundance of fish and game at all seasons, and
winter lasting only four months. I have seen there a
kind of fishing that is very good sport, and can be
carried on in winter, through the ice, as well as in
summer ; it is fishing for herring, which abound there.
What are also worth seeing in that country, are several
small lakes. of a league or two leagues round, in the
midst of the cleared lands, bordered all round with
prairies, with little woods near, from out of which
numbers of deer come to feed ; so that by lying in wait.
one may be sure to be able to shoot some of them ; and
at the proper season one sees all these lakes crowded
with water fowl. Wild turkeys and other feathered game

are to be found in the fields. But I could not describe to you all the beautiful places in those countries, nor the good things to be found there, and at the same time be brief, as I intend to be.

CHAPTER III.

DESCRIPTION OF THE LAND OF WHICH WE HAVE KNOWLEDGE.

I think it will be to the purpose to give you here some description of the land we are acquainted with, varying as it does in different places, either as to form or as to its nature and quality.

I will not speak to you here of the first land one meets with on coming from France, because it is not worth speaking of in comparison with that elsewhere ; indeed to speak correctly, it is not land but great rocks, horrible to behold.

From *Percée* Island, which is at the mouth of the great river, as far as to where you are opposite Tadousac, on the south side, which the ships keep to on their way up to Quebec, all the land appears to be high, and the greater part of it lofty mountains. Those called the *Notre Dame* Mountains, rise above a part of this line of coast ; and it is said that they are hardly ever free from snow, and consequently uninhabitable ; not but what there are between those mountains and the bank of the great river, four, five, and in some places eight leagues of level land, and the whole country is intersected by fine rivers. Still I deem it quite unfit for habitation, all

except *Gaspé*, which I consider very well adapted for a
settlement; there is a bay there that extends far back
into the land, and forms a basin fit for ships to take
shelter in.

At the head of the bay the land seems very well
adapted for a settlement. Besides there is very good
cod fishing in these parts.

There are also three other fine harbours, ten or twelve
leagues lower down, namely, *Percée* Island, Bonaventure
and Miscou, from all of which harbours ships go to fish
for cod every year) It would be a good place for a
settlement, on the score of facility of communication
with Quebec, access to which in small vessels is easy.

' There, to the right, is seen the Island of Anticosti, of
which I shall not speak to you, not having been to it;
only I have heard it said that there is very good land on
it, as well as on the north shore of the great river, from
Tadousac downwards, where one meets with many fine
rivers, whose waters are deep and abound with fish,
especially salmon; there are prodigious quantities of
this fish there, according to the accounts given to me
by those who have been there.

From Tadousac to a place seven leagues from Quebec,
called Cape *Tourmente*, the country is quite uninhabi-
able, being nothing but rocks, quite steep and high. I
have observed only one place along there, and that is
Saint Paul's Bay, about half way up, and opposite to
Coudres Island, which looks well as one passes it, as
do the islands between Tadousac and Quebec, all of
which are fit for settlement. I do not describe any
of them in particular, my intention being only to give
you a short sketch of the country as a whole, and of
some of the principal places in it.

4

The south shore, from Tadousac to Quebec, is very beautiful; and the land is low, and appears from the trees with which it is covered, to be very good. There are several fine rivers all full of fish, and of wild fowl in their season; there are also fine prairies along the coast, so that there are numbers of deer in those parts.

From Quebec to Three-Rivers, on the south side, also the land is fine enough; but it is high until you come to six or seven leagues below Three-Rivers, where it begins to be low, and fine, and level, and so continues until you come to the Iroquois country. These lands are very good, intersected by rivers, and adorned with lakes here and there. Many prairies are to be met with also not only along the great river, around the lakes, and on the little rivers, but also in the interior; so that there is abundance of game there, birds as well as animals.

On the north shore, from Cape *Tourmente*, which is seven leagues below Quebec, to *Carouge*, which is three leagues above it there are settlements along the line of the great river; from Carouge to the River Saint Anne, which is about seventeen leagues further up the river, the land is good enough, but the approach to it is not good, because the greater part of the shore is stony. But there are fine rivers there, and prairies in some places. From the River Saint Anne to Three-Rivers, which is about ten leagues, the land is very fine, and lies low, the beach along the great river is sandy or grassy, the forests are very fine, and easy to clear away.

Between Quebec and Three Rivers, there are no islands, except two little ones, of about one league round each, which are near the main land on the north side of the river; they are called Saint Anne Island and Saint Eloi Island.

Between Three-Rivers and Montreal, there are many beautiful islands, most of which are still without names ; among the most considerable, is one called Saint Ignace Island, close to which there are nearly a score which are called the Richelieu Islands. I shall not dwell upon their beauty, nor upon the good fishing and shooting to be got among them ; I should become too prolix if I allowed myself to enter into particulars about all the places I mention. I will content myself with simply saying that there are many prairies on these islands.

An immense quantity of nettles fit for making hemp from, grows in the woods here ; the Huron and Iroquois Indians use it in making various things, such as sacks, nets, and necklaces ; great quantities of it are to be found in many places in this country.

. After these, other islands called the Bouchard Islands, are to be seen ; and higher up the river are the Saint John Islands, then *les Iles Percées*, * Sainte Thérèse Island, Saint Paul's Island, and many others not yet named, all very beautiful and fit for settlement, and moreover abounding in fish and game and in prairies.

On the north shore the country is very fine, and all along the river there are prairies ; and the land here is watered by many small rivers.

The River *des Prairies* is a large river that joins the River Saint Lawrence, six leagues below the settlement of Montreal, and twenty-four leagues above Three-Rivers. This river is made use of as the way to the Huron country, although it is a much longer and more difficult way than the other, in order to avoid the Iroquois, who live beside the great lake, called Iroquois Lake, through which the River Saint Lawrence flows.

---

* Now called the Boucherville Islands.—Translator.

I shall not describe the land to be found on either
side of this river, which flows from a northerly direction,
seeing that it would be inconvenient to settle there on
account of the rapids, or cascades of water there, which
prevent the river from being navigable for other vessels
than the little ones our Indians use, which can be trans-
ported from one place to another on a man's shoulders,
or on the shoulders of two men at the most. It is a
great pity; for there are fine tracts of country there that
would be well worth settling upon; particularly one
called *La Petite Nation*, which is between twenty and
thirty leagues above Montreal, and consists of about
twenty leagues of land along the river, the finest that
can be seen in an uninhabited country; for the Iroquois
have driven away the Indians who lived there. It is a
fine forest, full of small lakes and prairies, with a great
number of small rivers; all of these abound with fish and
game to an incredible amount. But what is most to be
wondered at, is the great number of deer that are to be
found there; for I know that some Frenchmen on their
way down from the Huron country. met with herds of
those animals, we call wild cows here, but which are
properly speaking large deer, in which they reckoned that
there were quite as many as from eight to nine hundred,
to say nothing of common deer, bears, moose, beavers,
otters, muskrats and many other kinds of animals. But
access to it is barred by a great rapid, which is at least
three leagues long. When I say barred, I mean that it is
so for the present; for when the country becomes inhabited, and the Iroquois have been subdued, means will
soon be found to render the access to it easy; and
besides, there is no lack of fine places for settlement
which cannot be taken up for some time to come.

And now it seems to me that I have said enough to make the country itself known; let me say in addition only a few words about the soil in it. Loam is to be found in some places; in others the earth is black, or sandy, or red, or stony; but all these soils are fertile enough; and to prove that they are so, I shall treat in the next chapter of the trees they produce.

CHAPTER IV.

OF THE TREES THAT GROW IN NEW FRANCE.

I can imagine that the curious reader is already beginning to wish to know what sorts of trees grow in these great forests, and whether they are all the same every where. What are they good for? can any use be made of them? are they large? are they tall? is their wood sound? he asks. All these questions, my dear reader, I will answer by describing them to you as simply and as truly as I can, trying to avoid any exaggeration, as I have done, and as I hope to continue to do, throughout this treatise; then you may judge for yourself what they are fit for, and what can be made of them. I shall not follow any order, but shall name them as they occur to my memory.

I begin with one which is the most useful of those here, and which we call pine, but which does not bear any fruit as pines in Europe do. These trees are of various sizes and heights; but they generally grow to fifty or sixty feet without branches. Their wood is used for making planks and boards which are very fine and good; and it is said that these trees would be very fit for making masts for ships,) Some of them are to be found sufficiently slight and tall for that purpose, and they grow very straight. There are great tracts of country quite destitute of them. The places where they grow are called pineries.

These trees yield quantities of gum : the Indians use it for paying the seams of their canoes, and it is used successfully in the dressing of wounds and sores, for which it is a sovereign remedy.

Cedars also grow here. Their leaves are flat, and their wood is soft, but almost imperishable, for which reason it is used here for making garden fences and beams in cellars. These trees have a good smell but as a general rule they are not sound ; still there are large ones to be found out of which articles of furniture might be made ; they yield a gum which when burned has a very good smell like incense. I do not know that it has any other quality.

There are fir trees here, as there are in France. The only difference I find in them is that most of them have little blisters on the bark full of a kind of liquid gum, that is quite aromatic and is used as a balsam for wounds, and not without good effect according to the report of those who have tried it. Many other things are said of it ; but I leave that to the Physicians.

There is another kind of tree here, called spruce ; it is much like the fir, but is better adapted for making masts for small vessels, such as sailing-boats, being stronger than fir. It is an evergreen.

The American or black larch or tamarac, has a harder and heavier wood, which is very good to build with ; it sheds its leaves in the autumn and puts forth new ones in the spring, which is not the case with the other soft wood trees. Its bark is rough. and does not yield any gum, in which it differs from the spruce which has plenty of it.

There is still another kind of these trees, which we call hemlock ; these are generally large trees, growing to a height of from thirty to forty feet without branches ; they have a coarse red bark ; their wood does not rot so soon as that of the others, for which reason it is used very generally for building purposes. The worst of this wood is that so much of it is found to be blighted blasted and has therefore to be cast aside. This tree grows everywhere, in good land and in bad ; it does not yield any gum.

I may state here that all the above mentioned trees grow in damp places only, with the exception of pine and hemlock, which grow in dry places as well as in damp ones.

There is another kind of tree called maple, which grows very large and high; its wood is very fine, but is used only for fuel and for making handles for tools ; for which last purpose it is very well adapted. being very smooth and strong. When gashes are made in these trees in the spring, there runs out from them a quantity of water which is sweeter than sugar and water, or at least more pleasant to drink.

The tree called cherry birch grows big and high, and very straight. Its wood is used for making household furniture and the stocks of firearms. It is red inside, and makes the most beautiful work of any wood in these parts. It does not bear any fruit. It has been named cherry birch because its bark resembles that of the wild cherry tree in France.

There is also a kind of beech tree here that bears

beech-nuts like those in France. Its wood is good and fine, but is used only for fuel.

Two sorts of oaks are found here, the wood of one of which is of a more open grain than that of the other, and is therefore more fit for the making of household furniture and for joiner's and carpenter's work, while the other is good for ship building purposes. These trees grow tall and large and straight, particularly in the neighbourhood of Montreal.

There are also two kinds of ash, one of which is called white ash, and the other red ash. both of which grow tall and straight ; their wood is good and fine.

There are elms also, which grow large and high, and the wood of which is excellent ; wheelwrights in this country make great use of it.

There are also walnut trees, of two sorts ; those of one sort bear large hard nuts, but their wood is very soft and is not used for making anything but wooden shoes, for which it is very good ; of this kind there are plenty about Quebec and Three Rivers, but not many further up the country ; those of the other sort bear little round nuts, with soft shells, like those in France; but their wood is very hard and of a dark colour within; one begins to meet with them at Montreal, and there are quantities of them in the Iroquois country. The Indians even make excellent oil out of the nuts.

Another kind of tree, which we call the red-flowering or swamp maple, is something like the maple mentioned above; but the wood is softer, and is used only for fuel.

There is also the paper or canoe birch tree, very tall and large ; our Indians use its bark for covering the framework of their canoes and the roofs of their portable huts with ; it can be rolled up like canvas, and when it is unrolled

and stretched over rails supported on pickets stuck in
the earth, one can shelter oneself under it as one would
under a tent ; the Indians make dishes and other little
utensils for their own use out of it also ; the wood of
this tree is very good and very sound, but no use is
made of it here.

Aspens of all sorts are found here also ; that is to say
large and small ones ; they serve as food for the beavers,
which are very fond of their bark.

There are other trees called bass wood trees, or by
some people lime or linden trees. The wood of these
trees is white and very soft, and decays quickly in water ;
their bark serves our Indians for many purposes ; that
of the large trees is used by them for making a kind of
cask, in which they put their grain and other things ;
the bark of the smaller trees serves them for tying things
with, and they even get from it a kind of hemp of which
they make ropes.

There are chestnut trees and mulberry trees here,
which are to be found only in the Iroquois country. As
for the chestnut trees, they abound there, and produce
as good fruit as those in France ; the trees, however,
are much larger and taller.

Many other trees are to be seen in that Iroquois
country that we have not any of here in our neighbourhood, and the names of which I do not know ; but I
know very well that some of them have wood of a red
colour and very well adapted for making household
furniture with.

There are also in these parts abundance of hazel trees,
which bear plenty of nuts ; elder, hawthorn, producing
haws larger than those in France and much better tasted,
and plum trees, bearing red plums the size of damsons,

5

that have a pretty good taste, but yet not so good as that of those in France.

There are willows and alders in abundance.

Gooseberry bushes are to be found here that bear gooseberries of two kinds, one like those in France, the other full of prickles.

There are also red currant bushes.

There are also trees that we call wild cherry or bird cherry trees, bearing two or three sorts of small fruits ; their taste is not disagreeable, but they are very small ; the trees never grow to be large.

There are still some other small fruit trees like these, which it is not worth while to speak of, being as they are but of little consequence.

As I am on the subject of fruit bearing plants, I must not omit to tell you of the raspberry and strawberry plants that are to be found in incredible abundance all over this country ; the ground is quite covered with them, and they grow up in spite of you. and they produce so great a quantity of fruit that in the season the supply of it is inexhaustible. The berries grow larger and taste better than those in France.

Small fruit of another sort of the size of large peas, is found here ; it is called blueberry, and has a very good taste ; the bushes on which it grows are not more than a foot high ; they do not grow everywhere, but there are places in which there are great quantities of them.

The blackberry bushes of this country produce fruit that is almost as well tasted as our blackberries in France, but it is not so large.

There are numbers of small fruits here whose names I do not know, and which are not very exquisite but are eaten for want of better.

There are also plenty of wild vines that bear grapes. The grapes are not so large as those on our vines in France, nor are the bunches so full of them ; but I think if they were cultivated they would not differ from them in any respect   The juice of these grapes is rather tart, and makes a coarse wine that stains very much, and is generally better after than it is during the year in which it is made

Some persons have planted in their gardens grape vines brought from France, which have borne very fine and good grapes.

No trees from France have been planted here yet, except some apple trees, which bear very good apples, and plenty of them ; but there are very few of these trees.

***

CHAPTER V.

NAMES OF THE ANIMALS TO BE MET WITH IN NEW FRANCE.

In order to keep the promise I made in my first chapter, that I would treat of each thing by itself, I will give you in this chapter the names of the animals in Canada, and the places where they are usually met with ; for as you know, all things are not found in one and the same place.   By this means I will save you from that confusion of ideas which comes of things being treated of too generally, or as it were by wholesale.

Let us begin then by the most common and the most widely distributed of all the animals of this country, which is the elk, called here the moose.   These animals are generally larger than large mules, and have much the same shaped heads. The difference is that the males have branching horns, like those of stags except that they are flat. These fall off every year and are renewed, increasing by one branch or prong yearly. Their flesh is good, and is easily digested and never disagrees with any one. The skin is taken to France to be made into buff; the marrow is a specific for nervous pains. It is said that the hoof of a left foot is good for epilepsy, This animal has very long legs and is very agile; it has cloven hoofs and is without a tail; it defends itself by striking with its fore-legs, like a stag.

The cariboo is an animal about as high as an ass, but very agile. The males have cloven hoofs, and open them so wide when running, that in winter they do not sink in the snow, however deep it may be. They have also branching horns, round and pointed. Their flesh is good to eat, tender and delicate.

The bears are black; there are no white ones in these parts; the skins of the cubs are of some value for muffs; they are not mischievous if not provoked; their flesh is good to eat; the fat when melted becomes like oil and is good for scrofula; they pass six months without coming out of the places where they hide themselves; they usually retire into the hollow of trees; they are very fond of acorns, and that is why there are such numbers of them in and near the Iroquois country; they are carnivorous, and kill and eat pigs when they catch them in lonely places.

The animals called here wild cows are a kind of deer; the males have horns like those of deer, and shed them every year; they have cloven hoofs; they are as large as large deer; their flesh is tender; they generally go in herds, and are not to be met with everywhere; none are to be seen below, but many above Three Rivers; the further up towards the Iroquois-country one goes the more there are of them.

There are also animals that we call deer, of the same shape as those in France, but smaller, and with hair of a lighter colour; none of them are to be found below, but many above Montreal; further up the country they are innumerable.

As for the animals called buffaloes, they are to be found only in the country of the Outaoüaks. about four or five hundred leagues from Quebec, towards the west and north.

There are wolves of two kinds : One kind is the lynx, whose skin is good for making furs; these animals abound in the north, but there are very few of them near our settlements. The other kind is the wolf proper, which is not nearly so large as that in France, nor so vicious, but has a finer skin ; these are carnivorous, and prey upon other animals in the woods; and when they find our little dogs in lonely places they devour them ; there are few of them about Quebec. They become more and more common as one goes up the country.

There are also numbers of foxes all over the country. As I do not see any difference between them and those in France, I shall not say anything more about them, except that black ones are to be met with sometimes, but very seldom.

There is another kind of animal smaller than a fox, that climbs up trees; it is called child of the devil ; it is very fond of flesh, and much given to the killing of elks ; its flesh is good.

There are also martens, but they are all russet-haired ; here are no black ones to be seen.

There are animals called wild cats, not that they at all resemble other cats, but because they climb up trees; they are much larger than our cats, and are generally very fat; their flesh is good; the Indians make dresses of their skins.

There are porcupines; the Indians use their quills, which are very long, hollow and pointed at both ends, in the making of numbers of little articles that serve them for ornament, as lace does with us. The flesh of this animal is good.

There is another animal here a little smaller, called a ground-hog; it lives in the ground, and makes a den like the fox; its flesh also is good.

There are numbers of hares here; they are not so large as those in France; it is a remarkable thing that in summer they are grey and in winter they are white, so that they change colour twice a year

There are other animals here called skunks. These animals do not run fast but when one of them finds itself pursued it voids urine, and that urine is so offensive that it taints the air in all the neighbourhood; and for a fortnight or even three weeks afterwards, one may perceive its odour on approaching the place; this animal strangles fowls when it can catch them.

There is here a much smaller animal that also makes war upon the poultry; it is called a fisher, because it goes in the water as well as on land.

There are four kinds of squirrels here, one of which is russet-haired, like those in France, while another is smaller and has two black and two white stripes along its back; those of the latter kind are called Swiss squirrels. There are some of a third kind, that are large and ash-coloured, and are called flying squirrels because they actually fly from one tree to another by the aid of certain membranes that are extended when they stretch out their legs; they never fly upwards like birds, but, always along or downwards; they are delicate and pretty. The fourth kind is the black squirrel; these are larger than any of the others; their skins are very fine, and the Indians use them to make dresses of; this is a pretty animal and a curious one; but it is only to be found in the Iroquois country.

And now let me mention the amphibious animals, that live in the water and on land, such as beavers, otters and muskrats.

The beaver is an animal with very short legs, that lives in the water and on land; it has a large flat tail, the skin of which is like scales; you know that its fur is used in the manufacture of hats, and is the staple article of the trade of this country. These animals multiply rapidly; their flesh is as tender as mutton; some of their parts are in request with the apothecaries. Homely as they are, these animals possess wonderful skill, not only in making dwellings for themselves on land and in the water, but also in building dams; for they are dexterous enough to stop the course of small rivers, by making dams across them that their waters cannot break through, and by this means to flood considerable extents of country, which serve them for ponds to live and enjoy themselves in. The Indian hunters have all the trouble in the world to break these dams. The beavers in the north are worth more and have better fur than those in the south.

As for otters, they are usually found in lakes; some of them have pretty good skins.

The muskrat is an animal that lives in the water, and is valued for some of its organs which have an odour of musk during the months of April and May ; its skin is like that of the rabbit in colour as well as in size ; its flesh is good.

There are also weasels, and moles, and field and other mice.

So much for the animals of the country.

Of those that have been brought from France there are oxen and cows ; the oxen are employed in ploughing the land, and in drawing wood over the snow in winter. There are also pigs in great number ; of sheep, there are not so many ; then there are dogs, cats and rats ; these are the animals that have been brought from France, and they thrive well in this country.

After having mentioned all the animals in the country, let me say a word about the reptiles that are to be found in it.

Snakes of various kinds are to be seen ; there are some with black and white, and others with green and yellow skins ; they are harmless, or, at any rate they have not yet been found to be otherwise ; the longest are about an ell long, but there are not many so long as that ; the further up the country one goes the more numerous one finds them. In the Iroquois country there is another kind, called rattle snakes ; these are dangerous, they sometimes bite the Indians, who would soon die of their bites if it were not for their knowledge of a plant growing in that country, which being applied to the wound in the shape of a poultice draws the venom out of it.

There are lizards also, and other such little animals; and as for toads, why I have never seen such large ones in France.

There are frogs of several kinds ; I have seen them of three kinds, one consisting of green ones, as large as a

horse's foot, that are to be found on the banks of the
great river; they bellow in the evenings like oxen, and
many of our newly arrived people have been deceived
into thinking they heard wild cows, and would not
believe those who told them it was only frogs they heard;
they may be heard at a great distance; the Huron
Indians eat them and say they are very good. There
are others like those in France, and they are the most
numerous. I have seen some of a third kind, quite like
common frogs in every respect, except that they have
tails; I have never seen any of these elsewhere than in
one place, alongside of a small river, but there I saw
more than one hundred.

———-

CHAPTER VI.

NAMES OF THE BIRDS IN NEW FRANCE.

While giving you the names of the birds in this country, I shall not tell you of those that are to be met with
in the entrance of the gulf, such as cormorants, penguins,
coots, sea-gulls, and a number of others that belong to
the sea rather than to the land; but I will name to you
only those that are near to us, and that we kill every day,
such as swans, *outardes*, brant geese, wild geese, cranes,
ducks, teal, divers of more than ten kinds, ernes, bitterns,
herons, woodcock, snipe, tatlers, plover, ring plover
and sandpipers.) All the above named are river birds,
seeing that although they are not all to be found in the
rivers, they are all to be found along the shores of rivers.

6

The whole of this country is full of this kind of game in its seasons, that is to say in the spring and in the autumn.

As the *outarde* is not a bird that is common in France, I shall give a short description of it, because it is the most common of the river game here; in shape it is just like a grey goose, but it is much larger; its flesh is not so tender as that of the geese we see here in Canada which are quite white, with the exception of the tips of . the wings and of the tail, which are black; but as for the flesh of the geese in France, that is far from being comparable in flavour to the flesh of our *outarde*.

The other birds are the eagle, the turkey and birds of prey of more than fifteen kinds, of which I do not know the names, with the exception of the hawk and the falcon.

The female eagle has a white head and a white tail, and is called a little nun.

The wild turkey is not to be found at Quebec, nor at Three-Rivers, nor at Montreal; but in the Iroquois country and in the country in which the Hurons used to live, there are great numbers of them; their flesh is much more tender than that of the domestic turkey.

There are three kinds of partridges in this country; those of one kind are white, and are only to be met with in winter; they are feathered down to their toes; they are very pretty, and larger than those in France; their flesh is tender. There are other partridges that are quite black, with red eyes; they are smaller than those in France. and their flesh is not so good to eat; but they are beautiful birds, and are not very common. There are also grey partridges, that are as large as fowls; these are very common and very easy to kill, for they hardly

try to escape from any one ; their flesh is very white and
dry.

There are birds of another kind called wild pigeons ;
these are almost as large as tame pigeons, and their plumage is ash-coloured ; the male birds have red plumage
on their breasts, and they taste very well. There are
prodigious numbers of them, and forty or forty-five of
them have been killed at one shot; not that this is usual,
though killing eight, ten or twelve at a shot is a common
thing ; they generally come in the month of May and go
away in the month of September; they are to be found
every where in this country. The Iroquois take them in
nets as they fly, sometimes by three hundred or four
hundred at a time.

There are also great numbers of starlings which flock
together in September and October, and quantities of
thrushes. robins, ortolans, and an infinite number of other
little birds whose names I do not know.

There are swallows, martins, jays and magpies ; but
they are not like those in France, for they are ash-coloured
and ill-shaped.

Screech owls and other owls are to be seen here as
well as raven and crows ; also golden-winged and other
woodpeckers, and little birds as red as fire all over and
others that are red and black, others all yellow, and
others again all blue

Humming-birds, which are the smallest of all, are
a'most all green, except the male birds, which have red
throats.

The birds that have been brought hither from France
are fowls, turkeys and tame pigeons.

CHAPTER VII.

At the entrance into the gulf, young whales are to be seen, and it is even said that there are full grown whales there.

There are quantities of cod fish there also, and these may be caught to within ten leagues of Tadousac.

From there to Montreal, great number of white porpoises are to be found, from which, if they could be caught, oil could be made.

One sees extraordinary numbers of them between Tadousac and Quebec, leaping about in the river; they are very long and large, and at least a barrel of oil may be reckoned on to be got from each, according to experience with some found aground.

(There are also numbers of seals about Tadousac and lower down; the oil from them is very good, not only for burning in lamps but for many other purposes; they are very easily caught, and their skins serve for many uses.

There are quantities of salmon and trout from the entrance of the gulf to Quebec; none are to be found at Three-Rivers, nor at Montreal, but numbers of them in the Iroquois country.

There is an abundance of mackerel, but it is to be found only at *Percée* Island.

Herring strikes in at many places; at *Percée* Island.

at Tadousac, and at rivers elsewhere, it goes in schools as in Europe.

Sturgeon is to be taken from Quebec upwards ; and in all the great lakes there are great quantities of it ; very few little ones are to be seen there ; but all large sturgeons of four, six and eight feet long ; I have seen them taken in abundance in front of the settlement at Montreal, when there were men there who were fond of fishing. It is very good when salted, and keeps for a very long time. I have eaten some that had been salted for two years and was as good as it would have been four days after it was taken.

Shad is more abundant at Quebec than at any other place ; there are prodigious quantities there in spring, which is the season for taking them.

Bar is a fresh water fish ; quantities of it are taken at Quebec and Three-Rivers ; I never heard of any being taken at Tadousac or at Montreal ; the flesh of this fish is very good, and it is not a bony one.

The cat fish that is so common and so plenty in all parts of this country, is a fish without scales, having a head bigger than the rest of its body, and no bones besides the back bone ; its flesh is white and tender, though it is one of the fattest of the fish in this country ; it is generally from a foot and a half to two feet long ; it is caught with hook and line and is very good salted.

There are also plenty of smelts in the autumn at Quebec, as well as at Tadousac.

Loach are to be found at Tadousac, and quantities of fish of other kinds that I do not know the names of.

Eels are caught at Quebec in greater abundance than at any other place, in the month of September and in the beginning of October ; they are larger and better tasted than those in France. I have seen some as big as a man's leg; the flesh is tender and delicate, and keeps very well when salted; they are taken in weirs, and in such quantities as cannot be conceived of without having been seen

The fish that are to be found in the small lakes and rivers are pike, carp of several kinds, perch, bream, small trout, *dorées, ouchigans*, bass and a flat fish of another kind that has no french name any more than the last, small but very good, and another called white fish; these are the most common ones, and they are to be met with every where.

The pike are generally very large here. The carp, of whatever kind they may be, are not very good unless they are fried in oil; their flesh is flabby.

Of all these kinds of fish there are plenty in all the small lakes and rivers.

In the great lakes, there are quantities of fine large fish of different kinds that have not yet any names among us Frenchmen, but still are delicious eating. I shall not describe them; they are too far away from us for that.

It would be very difficult to give the names of all the fish that are to be taken in a great country like this. From time to time some are taken, the like of which had not been seen before. Crabs are also to be found in the little rivers.

I was going to forget to give you a description of a fish that we call the armed fish *(poisson armé)*; it is about two feet and a half or from that to three feet long; it is quite round and is from six to eight inches in circonference; it is of about the same size from end to end; it has a very hard shell, so hard that one could not pierce

through it with a sword; its snout is about eight inches
long, and as hard as a bone; it is armed with three rows of
teeth on each side that are as pointed as awls; the flesh
is not worth much for eating. It is very easy to take,
but it is scarce.

CHAPTER VIII.

NAMES OF THE CEREAL AND OTHER PLANTS THAT GROW IN THIS COUNTRY FROM SEEDS BROUGHT FROM EUROPE.

During my visit to France I met with many persons
who asked me whether any grain was grown in New
France, and whether any bread was eaten here. That is
why I write this chapter, to undeceive those who imagine
that we live upon roots only in this country, as people
do in the Island of Saint Christopher. (They shall know
then that wheat grows very well here, and bread is made
of it as fine and as white as any in France. Rye grows
up here more than is desirable. All kinds of barley and
peas thrive very well here, and one never sees any of
those worm-eaten peas full of weevils that one sees in
France Lentils, vetch, oats and millet grow quite well;
broad beans grow well also; but there are some years
when great flies feed upon them when they are in flower.
Buck-wheat grows here also; but it sometimes happens
that it is touched by frost before it is ripe. Hemp and
flax grow finer and higher here than in France.)
The kinds of grains cultivated by the Indians, and
which they had before we came to the country are large
millet, or Indian corn and kidney beans, they raise also

pumpkins of a different kind from those in France ; they
are smaller, and are not so hollow, and the flesh is firmer
and less watery, and has a better taste; turnsole, from
the seeds of which they make a very nice oil with a very
good taste, and a plant from which they make their
tobacco, for Indians are great smokers, and cannot do
without tobacco. Cultivating these things is what the
farming done by the Indians consists of.

All sorts of turnips and radishes, beet-roots, carrots,
parsnips, salsify, and other roots grow perfectly well and
very large. All sorts of cabbages also grow here in per-
fection, with the exception of cauliflowers, which I have
not seen here yet.

As for other plants, sorrel, chards of all shapes,
asparagus, spinage, lettuces of all sorts, chervil, parsley,
endive, burnet, onions, leeks, garlic, chives, hyssop,
borage, ox-tongue, and generally all sorts of plants that
grow in gardens in France, melons, cucumbers, water-
melons and gourds grow very well here.)

As for flowers, none have yet been brought from
France except roses, carnation, tulips, white lilies, holly
hocks, anemones and lark spur, which do just as well
here as in France.

As for wild plants, I shall not undertake to give you
the names of them in this place, except those of such as
are most commonly met with here in the woods. The
chervil has a larger leaf and a much thicker stalk than
that in France, and is well tasted enough. The garlic is
smaller than that in France ; and great numbers of small
onions like chives grow all along the great river. There
is samphire here, and wild parsley, just like Macedonian
parsley ; there is also angelica in the prairies, and pur-
slane grows of itself on land that has been cleared but

not sown ; but it is not so fine as that we cultivate. In the prairies there is to be found a plant that we call vetch which makes excellent hay, and another that we call wild pea ; there is more of these about Three-Rivers and Montreal, where the tide does not ebb and flow than about Quebec. Hops grow here of themselves also, and very good beer is made with them. Poison hemlock grows wonderfully well here, and so does hellebore ; maiden hair grows here in abundance ; several kinds of ferns are found here, and nettles, of which thread is made and very good rope, also melilot, or sweet clover, and reeds and rushes along the rivers.

There are also many kinds of flowers, the chief of which are, yellow lilies, wild roses that are not double, a red flower that we call cardinal flower, a species of lily, lilies of the valley, violets that are single and have no perfume. I do not know the names of the others ; but those who have been to the Iroquois country have told me that it is wonderful to see the quantity and variety of the beautiful flowers to be found there.

CHAPTER IX.

OF THE INDIANS OF NEW FRANCE, AND OF THEIR WAY OF LIVING.

All the Indians in New France are nearly alike, particularly as respects their clothing and the fashioning of it ; but as they differ in their ways of living and in their languages, we shall divide them into two classes, in which all the tribes in these countries shall be included, that is to say Algonquins and Hurons.

7

All the tribes that live on the north side, below as well as above, are Algonquins, and do not differ very much from each other in language, except as the inhabitants of Poitou differ from those of Provence or of Gascony ; and on the South side there are the Abenakis, the Acadians, the Sokokis,and all the Wolf tribe who are rather Algonquins than Hurons. In the upper country, the Ottawas, the *Nez-percés* and all those other large tribes, almost all speak Algonquin

On the other hand, the *Petun* tribe, the neutral tribe, all the Iroquois. and the *Andastoés* speak the Huron language, although the dialects are very different, as Spanish, Italian and French differ from Latin. But between the Huron and Algonquin languages, there is as much difference as there is between Greek and Latin.

The Algonquins are rovers, and live by hunting and fishing only, not knowing what it is to cultivate the ground ; and this is the case with all the tribes whose language has any affinity with the Algonquin language, on the contrary, the Hurons, the Iroquois, and all the tribes whose language has any affinity with the Huron language are sedentary, have villages, lay out fields, cultivate the soil, trade with other tribes, are more civilized, and have as it were officers among them for all sorts of affairs.

Let me describe the way of living of the Algonquins, after which I will speak of that of the Hurons.

The Algonquins, as I have said, are rovers, and live by hunting and fishing ; and for these purposes they have small vessels, called here canoes, made of white birch bark and strengthened inside by semi-circles of cedar wood ; and this is done so well and neatly that one man can carry one of these small vessels when he has to go

through the woods from one river to another ; and yet he
can embark in it with his wife and children, his arms, his
house and all his luggage. There are canoes of two,
three, four and five fathoms long.

Their houses usually consist of three pieces of white
birch bark, of about an ell wide and from three to four
ells long each, which can be folded up, like a painting
when it comes from the painter; when they halt for the
night they stretch these pieces of bark over three or four
round poles, placed so as to come together in a point
over head, so that the hut is round. large at the bottom
and contracting towards the top. It is usually the
woman who puts up the tent, unloads the canoe, lights
the fire, and prepares the supper, while the man goes and
takes a turn in the woods, to see if he can find something to kill. The woman has also to make the beds,
for which purpose she goes and cuts a lot of branches
from the nearest fir trees and spreads them upon the
ground to lie upon ; it is the woman also who has to cut
and bring in all the wood that may be required for fuel
for the house. When the men have killed any animal, it
is for the women to go and fetch the meat ; for they act
as porters for the men ; they skin the animal, they stretch
the skins out to dry and dress them afterwards to make
clothes of ; for our Indians do not go naked, as those of
the Island of Saint Christopher do, only they do not
cover their arms, except when the weather is very cold.

Generally speaking, the Indians, both men and women,
are very well made ; and one sees very few among them
having natural defects, such as squinting, being hump-
backed, or even being lame, unless as the result of
accident.

They are swarthy ; but new-born children are as white

as French ones, that swarthy colour only coming to them as they grow up. The men have no beards, and they all have coarse black hair, which both men and women grease very often. The Algonquins generally wear their hair very long.

They are by nature timid, cruel, insincere, compliant, ungrateful, especially the Algonquins, and impudent beggars; but the worst fault I see in them, is that they are extremely vindictive and will cherish for twenty years a resolve to be avenged, without letting it appear, but still always looking out for some chance or opportunity of having some pretext by way of justification It is not their way to let their ill will appear openly, or to fight when they meet, or hand to hand, as is done in Europe. A man who had done that would be odious among them; and as they are glad to have opportunities for revenging themselves upon their enemies without being blamed for it, that is one of the reasons why they are so passionately fond of getting drunk, thinking that when they have struck or killed any one in a drunken fit, that is no disgrace to them, because they can say that it was the liquor did it, not they; yet in their hearts they are delighted at having revenged themselves; whence it comes that an Indian seldom or never drinks but to get drunk and then execute revenge upon some one who has displeased him, or to gratify some other brutal passion, as for instance to ravish a girl or a woman. This our Bishop knows very well; and it is this knowledge that has made him so zealous in his opposition to those who gave the Indians liquor with which they immediately made themselves drunk, whence arose grievous troubles that were very shocking to good and pious people; for it is very certain that Indians do not drink for the pleasure of drinking, nor yet because they feel the want of liquor, but always with some bad intent; and this is so true that no one had ever seen or heard of such bad things among the Indians as have been done since intoxicating liquors have been given to them; for Indians are not by nature capable of great wickedness, as Europeans are; they do not even know what it is to swear; and although there are among them some who are thieves, they never steal boldly, or even with address, at least the Algonquins, although they are not wanting in intelligence.

The Indians in general are quick witted, and dullness and boorishness, such as we see among our peasants in France, are very rarely to be seen among them. They stand more in awe of reprimands from their parents or chiefs than people in Europe do of the rack or the gallows; and you see no want of order among them, although the fathers and mothers have no punishments for their children, nor the chiefs for their inferiors, except words of reproof; and I have seen some who have poisoned themselves, while others have hanged themselves, either in consequence of having received or for fear of receiving scoldings from their parents or their chiefs, for some little faults they had committed. Hence it follows that when a murder has been committed, the blame it cast not upon him who committed it, but upon the chiefs, who are compelled to make atonement to the relatives of the deceased; and as the making of it is very burdensome to the chiefs, the consequent embarrassment and humiliation of him who did the mischief is so great, that although nothing is said to him about it he generally banishes himself for the rest of his days; and the effect of this is to keep others in check.

They have great respect for their chiefs, and obey

them promptly, particularly when they are not given to vice; for when they are, they despise them very much, saying that a man who cannot govern himself is not fit to govern others.

They are not usually avaricious; this proceeds from the fact that those who live as they do (particularly the Algonquins) from hand to mouth do not care to store up any thing; they are not careful people

Liberality is held in estimation among them; whence it comes that the chiefs are generally poorer than the others; for when they first come forward they give away all that they have in order to gain the affections of their people, who make them many presents afterwards, and provide for them when they grow old.

None of them are braver than the others, and the best hunters are the best off

They do not know what it is to be served; each one does for himself.

The business of the Algonquin men is to hunt and fish, to go to war, to trade with distant tribes. to escort the women when they go to dangerous places, to make canoes, and that is all; every thing else has to be done by the women.

When they travel by water and their women are with them, the women paddle the canoes as well as the men.

Enough said about the Algonquins. Let us come now to the very different mode of life and customs of the tribes speaking the Huron language, such as those in the cantons of the Iroquois. They are, as I have already said, sedentary, and build villages. The men make the stockades and build the huts, which are like arbours but very high and large, and are covered from top to bottom with thick ash or elm bark : the best of these huts are covered with cedar bark, but such are scarce.

They cut down trees and clear land to make fields. When the wood has been burned off, the women do all the sowing, weeding, reaping and harvesting ; these also grind the corn, or rather pound it ; for the Indians have never had mills : having converted it into flour, they make bread with it, or they make a kind of hasty pudding, of flour and water, and some kind of seasoning when they have any, and this they call *Sagamité* ; for the women are the cooks and the bakers.

The men work also at making canoes, armour and nets ; but the women make the twine ; the men hold councils, deliberate about public affairs, that is to say those who are born to these functions ; for the rank of chief descends from father to son, and those who inherit it are taken into council as soon as they are of mature age and have shown themselves to be of sound intellect.

The men also hunt, fish and carry on wars ; the Iroquois do not trade with other Indian tribes, because they are hated by all of them ; the Hurons did so to a great extent and trafficked almost all over the country.

The men employ themselves also in making wooden dishes and spoons   It is they also who cultivate the fields of tobacco and make the calumets or pipes which they use in smoking ; the women make the earthen vessels and a number of small articles adapted to their usages, which I will not describe because they are not known in France.   They act as porters, and it is they who have to carry all that has to be carried.

I have been informed lately that the Iroquois men and women are served by their slaves, of whom they have a great number, both men and women.

CHAPTER X.

Let me say a few words about their marriages. When
a young man wishes to marry a girl he goes to see her,
caresses her, but never with any lack of decency, for
that would be considered among them an offence; he
speaks to her in private, and when he has succeeded in
winning her over, he makes her presents of things that
are most rare among them; and when all is settled he
goes to live, in the girl's hut, for the wife does not go to
live with her husband, but the husband goes to live with
his wife.

Among the Hurons it would not be considered a real
marriage, but rather an illicit connection, unless the
father and mother of the young man had gone to ask her
parents or other relatives for the girl whom they wished
to have for a wife for their son; and when this is done
some valuable present is made to the girl's relatives.

Although polygamy is not forbidden among them, one
rarely sees a man with two wives, particularly among the
Hurons or the Iroquois; but one sometimes does among
the Algonquins.

Divorce is not an odious thing among them Indians.
As a man can easily put away his wife, or a woman her
husband, (I speak of those who are not Christians) it is
done without any fuss; for when a woman wishes to put
away her husband, she has only to tell him to leave the
house, and he goes out of it without another word,
leaving her all he brought except his own clothes. In

the same way, when a man wishes to put away his wife
he withdraws himself after having told her that he is
about to leave her   The children, if they have any, all
remain with the wife.   These divorces happen but rarely
because each is on his or her guard and refrains from
displeasing the other for fear of bringing on a separation.

They are not much given to jealousy, least of all the
Iroquois.

They have games of different kinds among them, the
most common of which are a game with straws, a game
with a dish, and a third which they call *paquessen.*

The game with straws is played with little straws prepared for the purpose, which are divided at random into
three parcels very unequally. Our French people have
not yet been able to learn to play it well; it is full of
spirit and these straws are to the Indians what cards are
to us. .

The game with a dish is played with nine flattened
polished and rounded little pieces of bone, like peach
stones, black on one side and white on the other, which
are shaken and made to bounce about on a great wooden
dish, held with both hands and at last struck against the
ground ; the loss or gain depends upon a certain number
being found with the same coloured side uppermost.

The game called *paquessen* is almost the same, except
that the little bones are thrown into the air by hand so
as to fall upon a skin spread on the ground and serving
for a carpet ; the number all of one colour decides the
loss or the gain.

They feast with one another also, and after the following fashion. He who wishes to give a banquet causes a
large boiler to be put over a fire, or two, or three, according to the number of persons he wishes to entertain ;

into these boilers meat or fish is first put, and then Indian corn meal ; when the food is all cooked the giver of the feast sends and invites those whom he desires to have as guests ; they come, each bringing a plate and a spoon.   They enter the hut without saying a word ; and squat down on their hams like monkeys.   Meantime the host keeps singing until all the guests he invited have come in, and does not show them any ceremony.   When all have come in, he says : " I am giving a feast " ; or, if he wishes to gratify or to honour his son, or some other person, he makes it known by saying that such an one, naming him, gives the feast; then all those present cry ho ! by way of thanks ; he goes on to say that there are so many boilers, according to the number there ; they answer him again ·" ho !" the meat is that of such an animal, killed by such an one ; at each sentence the same answer " ho !" is made ; and so he goes on to tell all that the banquet consists of, and the same answer of " ho !" " ho " is always made to him.

Afterwards he says he wishes that certain of them, naming such, would sing ; and oftentimes he is the first to begin to sing, and the guests sing one after the other, to the number of those he has expressed a wish to hear.

They rise to sing, and put themselves into various postures and make various gestures while singing.   Their singing is not harmonious or sweet, but is like as if they were stirring themselves up to anger, and they even make signs sometimes of striking blows.   In these warlike songs they will relate their feats of prowess and tell of the men they have killed in battle, or of their intention to go to war in order to avenge the death of a relative or of some eminent man.   This binds the singer in honour to do so, and frequently those who sing afterwards

pledge themselves in their songs to follow him, and to
die with him.

After all have sung, the food is served out in this
way, that is to say, some *sagamité* is put into each guest's
plate, and if there is any meat it is distributed among
those the host desires most to honour and gratify, a piece
being given to each of them; the most delicate morsels
are given to the chiefs; the giver of the feast does not
eat anything, but sings while the others eat   If they are
Algonquins they may take their plates full of *sagamité*
home with them, but among the Iroquois and Hurons
this is not allowable and you must eat all you are helped
to, wherefore they bring very small plates with them; for
no one dares to go out of the hut before he has emptied
his plate, unless he makes a little present to the giver
of the feast, a knife, an awl or a plug of tobacco.   The
women are less often invited than the men, particularly
among the Iroquois and Hurons.

Very great feasts sometimes take place among them,
there was one during the time I was among the Hurons,
of the flesh of fifty deer, in fifty boilers.

They have also dances which are not at all like ours,
for they consist only of shaking the body in a certain
way, striking the feet against the ground and assuming
many postures, according to rule and in time to the music
of little drums or other instruments, which give out a low
dull sound; they keep time so well that one does not notice
any confusion or disorder, although there are sometimes
two hundred dancing together; they all stamp with their
feet at the same moment, and so well together that one
would think there was only one person dancing.

These dances generally take place on some occasion
of public rejoicing, as for a victory over an enemy, or for

a treaty of peace recently concluded; sometimes also they are got up by individuals at their homes and among their friends, but this is not very usual.

The sedentary tribes have officers for all sorts of affairs, whom they call chiefs; the principal ones are for the maintenance of order, others are for war, and there are others again whose only duty it is to make things known, and who serve for drummers and trumpeters; some of these go through the streets of the village in the evening or in the morning, calling out the names of those who have died during the past day or night; others are charged with the duty of making preparation for the burning of prisoners; others have to give notice when a Council is to be held, and warn those who are to attend it; the office of some others is to give notice all over the village of any merry making or public dance; and so on; and all without any confusion or want of order.

They have no religion, but they are very superstitious and have faith in their dreams; this is what gives the most trouble to the Jesuit Fathers who try to instruct them

They believe in the immortality of the soul, and say that after death it goes into a beautiful country; that before it can get there it has to pass a river where there is one who lays open the heads of all comers and takes out their brains, so that they no longer remember any thing.

They have a number of fables that they relate, and in each of them one may always remark some resemblance to some story in the Old Testament.

They have knowledge of spirits, and a great aversion to sorcerers; and when any one is accused of being a sorcerer, and it is thought that he is one, he is at once killed or burned as an enemy.

They are very charitable, and readily entertain stran-
gers· and travellers without expecting to be paid for so
doing ; and many of them will give up their beds, or, to
speak more correctly, the places where they lie down to
sleep, and give to eat of their best, and that often enough
to a man whom they have never seen before and will
perhaps never see again and who may go away without
thanking them. This is chiefly the case among the
sedentary tribes.

When any family is in want of food, there are chiefs
who go through the village and collect grain for their
sustenance ; and every one gives more or less, according
to his ability.

They are not niggardly towards each other ; when any
one has killed game or caught fish he is liberal with it,
either in the way of giving a feast or in that of sending
some of it to others.

They are pitiful and compassionate towards each
other.

They are very fond of their relatives, and mourn for
them long after they die ; when they bury them they place
with them that which they liked most during life and
what they themselves think the most precious of their
own goods.

Almost all of them have a pretty good amount of
common sense, and can reason very well ; that may be
seen in their councils, and in their speeches, which they
make often and on all sorts of occasions.

All the Indians in contact with Europeans become
drunkards, and this does great harm to our converts, for
of many who were good Christians several have fallen
away. The Jesuit Fathers have done all they could
to put a stop to this mischief ; for the Indians only

drink to make themselves drunk; and when they have begun to drink will give any thing that is asked for a bottle of brandy, in order to complete their intoxication.

The wars they wage against each other are not for conquests of territory, nor for personal aggrandizement, nor yet for the furthering of their interests in any other way, but merely for revenge and they do not make any professions to the contrary; for one will say, I am going to the war for the purpose of avenging the death of such an one; and that is why they treat their prisoners so cruelly, and never aim at less than the entire destruction of a hostile tribe.

CHAPTER XI.

THE WAY THE INDIANS MAKE WAR.

Those who go to war are not paid by any one; every one goes at his own expense, and has to supply himself with arms, food, ammunition and all other necessaries of war.

This is the way they call out their forces: a chief gives a feast (this is called putting on the kettle); to this feast he invites all the young men of his village, to whom he declares his intention to go to war to avenge the death of such or such an one; he exhorts such of them as are his friends to go with him; when he has said what he had to say on the subject and the banquet has been partaken of the guests retire; afterwards those who are inclined to accompany him, come one after the other and offer him their services, saying: "uncle so and so" (for that is how they usually address those whom they consider their betters) or, "my brother" (if they are equals) "I have come to tell you that I wish to take my chance with you in the war you have in view."

Then they all cause their stores of provisions to be prepared, and hold themselves in readiness for departure on the appointed day.

When a great enterprize is to be gone into it is deliberated upon long before by the Council of elders and the principal chiefs. and when the matter has been decided upon. and the person who is to conduct the expedition has been chosen, an officer goes through the village proclaiming that there is to be a war, and that all the young men are exhorted to go into the army. The chiefs of all-the villages that have sent delegates to the council cause the same thing to be done in those villages, and every young man who decides upon joining the expedition notifies the chief who is to lead it of his reso-lution to that effect as soon as it is formed.

Afterwards delegates are sent with presents to all their nearest allies, praying for their assistance in the under-taking. Thereupon these hold councils, at which they consider how many men they can contribute, or rather how many of their young men they can induce to join the main body.

.When they are all gathered together and are on the march they always have scouts that go in advance ; each village that has furnished men has chiefs in command of them ; and all the chiefs meet together frequently to con-sult about all sorts of things ; for they do not neglect any thing.

They frequently exhort their warriors to stand fast in battle and not run away, saying to them that men of . spirit and courage never run away.

There is no punishment among them for those who have run away, except that they are called cowards, but that only in a whisper.

When they have encountered the enemy and are fighting with him, the chiefs act the part of drummers and trumpeters, and cry out without ceasing : " have courage. young men, have courage, they are at our mercy, let no man run away." This heartens them very much, for they have great respect for their chiefs.

They are expert at taking by surprize and at laying ambushes ; and they do not go to work badly at making an honourable retreat when they find themselves too hard pressed ; they have given us experience of that.

They are spirited at first, but they do not hold out long. Neither are they good at fighting in the open field. They never begin to fight without first calling out all together, to astonish the enemy.

They are skilled in the handling of fire-arms, and fire very well with guns. They have simples in use among them that are very good for curing wounds, particularly gun shot ones.

They are very agile, and are capable of enduring very great fatigue ; they are very good walkers and runners, and have extraordinary skill in knowing where they are in the woods, and hardly ever lose themselves.

CHAPTER XII.

OF THE WAY THEY TREAT PRISONERS OF WAR.

When they have taken a prisoner, they first cut off one of his fingers, then they tie him by the arms and legs

with cords, except that on the march they leave his legs
free.

When they encamp at night they make him lie on his
back on the ground, into which they drive small stakes
one to the right of each hand and foot and one each to
the right of his neck and head, to these they tie him, so
that he cannot move, and this causes greater pain than
one would think, particularly in summer on account of
the stinging of the musketoes, for he is naked.

When they arrive at their village all the people come
out to meet them, and all are at liberty to do what harm
they choose to the prisoner, short of killing him. Then
you see some armed with knives, either cutting off his
fingers or making incisions in his arms, his back, or
other fleshy parts, the prisoner being quite naked, while
others are beating him with sticks. There are some
also who have rods, brambles and ropes' ends. With all
of these implements he is, as they say, caressed as he
comes in.

All this time, the prisoner must sing if he wishes to
appear to be a man of spirit and of courage ; and in fact
no Indian ever fails to sing all the time he is being
tortured ; but the song is a mournful one.

After he has got into the village he is led from hut to
hut ; and at the huts of the chiefs and every where else
he must sing.

After a day or two passed in these painful prelimina-
ries, the chiefs hold a council at which he is condemned
to death, or it is decided that his life shall be spared ; if
he is condemned to death. the Indian to whom he has
been given (for it is their custom to give each prisoner
for some one who has been killed in battle) that Indian,
I say, gives a feast, and when all his invited guests are

9

assembled he says to them : " Behold my son ", or " my nephew " (according to the degree of relationship to him of the person for whom the prisoner has been given to him) " who gives you his farewell feast." It is their custom to give a feast, which they call a farewell feast, before setting out upon a long voyage or journey. Then the prisoner sings, and after him some of the guests sing also.

After the guests have left, a hut to burn the prisoner in is got ready, large fires are made in it, and notice of the hour at which the burning of him will begin is sent through the village, so that all may be present.

When the hour has come, the poor victim is brought in, his arms above his elbows are tied to his body and his legs are fastened together by a rope about two feet long, so that he cannot take long strides. All the people are ranged along the two sides of the hut; and be it known to you by the way that they have no idea of such a thing as a chimney, and that they make their fires in the middle of the place.

So they leave a narrow path between the lighted fires, placed at intervals all along the middle of the hut, and the men ranged along its two sides, squatting on their hams like monkeys, and it is along this path that the prisoner has to run

Each man has a glowing firebrand or a red hot piece of iron in hand; when all is ready, some chiefs at one end of the hut with the prisoner call out aloud : " the prisoner is about to start, let every one be prepared to do his duty, but let him not be burned above the waist "

Then he is ordered to start, which he does at a run, or rather hobbling along as fast as he can between the fires and his tormentors, all of whom burn him as he passes, some on his legs, others on his thighs, and that with a degree of barbarity that is peculiar to them.

I declare to you that this is a perfect image of hell, for you see a great hut with fires all along the middle and full of smoke through which you can hardly see at all, for it is usually at night that this is done ; you see crowds of people, some seated, some standing, some acting the part of tormentors, some that of spectators, who scoff and laugh at the poor victim. In the midst of all you see a poor wretch quite naked and all scorched, a prey to the fury of these barbarians.

After they have made him go round the hut as many times as the Elders have ordered, which is usually ten or twelve, the night being nearly over, all the people go away, except some who remain to watch the prisoner until morning, when the execution is to be completed.

During that time he is tied to a post not far from a great fire in which hatchets are being heated red hot that are made use of to sear him while he is being interrogated from time to time as to the condition of his country and other things that they desire to be informed of; and if they see that he is hiding any thing they increase his torture, and in this way the remainder of the night is passed.

About sunrise next day the women are told to go and make fires at the place where the scaffold has been erected. I forgot to mention that as soon as a prisoner arrives, one is erected for him, whether it is intended that he shall be put to death or not, which scaffold they make him mount several times a day, so that he may be exposed to the view of the people.

When all these fires have been lighted, the victim is brought on to the scaffold, in the middle of which a great pole, or rather a very high stake has been set up ;

he is made to put his arms around this stake, and his
hands are then tied together; the cord with which his
legs are tied together is likewise passed round the stake;
so that he can turn round and round it.

He is there exposed and quite naked; there is a
ladder at each of the four corners of the scaffold, and
every one is at liberty to go upon the scaffold and torture
him. There is no lack of tormentors, on the contrary,
there are more than enough of them; we have observed
that the most cruel ones are cowards who never go to
the wars.

So they place him on the scaffold and burn him with
fire-brands, but with as much unconcern as if he were a
piece of wood.

After having tortured him in this way for two or three
hours, until he looks like a piece of charcoal, they flay
his head and take his scalp as they do to those they
kill in battle.

Then if there is any life left in the victim they cut his
throat with a knife, and split his chest open and take out
his heart; and if he has been a brave man, and has not
cried out while he was being tortured, some of them
drink his blood, in order that his courage may be com-
municated to them.

Then he is cut into four, and his quarters are thrown
into the gutter or sometimes they are cooked and eaten,
out of rage.

When the chiefs have decided to spare the life of a prisoner, and he to whom he has been given consents to its
being spared, (for he has more to say in the matter than
any other) he is unbound at once, the fact is made
public throughout the village, and thence forth he is well
treated, no one daring to hurt him any more, although

he is still looked upon as a slave and is obliged to serve him to whom he has been given in that capacity. His life is safe, provided he is not suspected of wishing to escape and does not fail to obey the orders that are given him; but if he is suspected of wishing to escape, his head is forthwith split open with an axe, and the same thing is done to him if he objects to obey orders.

If by God's grace we should some day become their masters, it would be easy to cure them of these barbarous customs and render them more civilized; for, as I have already said, they have very good common sense and are quite amenable to reason; and when once they are convinced of any thing they adhere strongly to their conviction; witness those poor Huron men and women taken prisoners by the Iroquois after having been taught and baptized by the Jesuit Fathers, who keep to their religion with such firmness and constancy in the midst of their enemies, and who put to shame many French libertines who have not behaved so piously among the enemy as those poor people who leap for joy when they meet with a Jesuit Father to whom they can make confession, and from whom they may receive the sacraments.

———

CHAPTER XIII.

ANSWERS TO QUESTIONS PUT TO THE AUTHOR WHEN HE WAS IN FRANCE.

During my stay in France, various questions on the subject of New France were put to me by worthy people. I think I shall oblige the curious reader by mentioning them here and by making a chapter of them and of my answers to them, which will give a good deal of information and knowledge to those who have an affection for this country and would like to come to it

I will begin with a very frequent one, which was whether vines grow well here. I have said already that there are plenty of wild vines and that some from France have been tried and have done pretty well. But why do you not plant vineyards? To this I answer that eating is more necessary than drinking, and therefore the raising of wheat has to be attended to, before the planting of vineyards; one can do better without wine than without bread. It has been as much as we could do to clear land and raise wheat, without doing any thing else.

Is wine dear? I answer that it is worth ten *sous* a quart; brandy is worth thirty *sous* a quart, and spanish wine is worth as much; the measures are the same as those of Paris.

Is wheat dear? Wheat is worth one hundred *sous* a *minot*, weighing sixty pounds; sometimes it is worth six francs.

Peas are worth half a crown a *minot*, and sometimes as much as four francs.

Are men's daily wages high? Twenty *sous* if fed during winter, and thirty *sous* if fed during summer.

Are there any horses in the country? I answer no.

Are there not prairies of which hay can be made? Do not oats grow there? Perfectly well, and there are beautiful prairies; but hay making is rather dangerous, particularly near the settlements at Three-Rivers and Montreal, and will continue to be dangerous so long as the Iroquois make war on us, for the mowers and hay makers are always in danger of being killed by them.

For this reason we make but little hay, although we have fine large prairies on which there grows very good grass for making it. But there is still another thing that pre-vents us from having horses, and that is that it would cost a good deal to bring them from France ; there are few people here who could afford the outlay, and besides it is feared that the Iroquois would kill them when they come, as they do our cattle, which would be very vexa tious to whoever had been to the expense of bringing them out. And besides, we are always in hopes that our good King will come to the assistance of this coun-try and will cause those rascally Iroquois to be destroyed.

Are there many settlers? To this question I cannot give any positive answer, except that I have been told that there are about eight hundred at Quebec : as for the other settlements there are not so many there.

Have the settlers many children? Yes, and they grow up well formed, tall and robust, the girls as well as the boys ; they are, generally speaking, intelligent enough, but rather idle, that is to say it is difficult to get them to attend to their studies.

Why is not hemp cultivated to a great extent, since it grows so well? I give the same reason with reference to hemp as I have given with reference to the vine, namely that until now we have thought only of wheat, as the most necessary thing. I will merely add that we are too few in number, but that when the Iroquois shall have been overthrown, want of settlers only will prevent us from having all that can be desired.

What is the ordinary beverage? Wine in the best houses. beer in some others ; there is another beverage called *bouillon*, that is in common use in all the houses ;

the poorer people drink water which is very good and very common in this country.

What are the houses built of? Some are built entirely of stone, and covered with boards or planks of pine ; others are built of wooden frame-work or uprights, with masonry between ; others are built wholly of wood ; but all the houses are covered, as I have said, with boards.

Is the heat very great in summer? It is about the same as in our province of *Dunis*.

Is the cold great in winter? There are some days when it is very severe, but it does not prevent one from doing what one has to do ; one puts on more clothes than usual, one covers one's hands with a kind of glove, called mittens in this country, and good fires are made in the houses, for wood costs nothing except for cutting it and bringing it on vehicles called sledges ; these slide upon the snow, and one ox can draw in this way as much as two could with a cart in summer. And, as I have already said, the air is very calm on most days, and little rain falls in winter. What I find most inconvenient here is that cattle must be fed in the stable for more than four months, on account of the ground being covered with snow during that time, but if the snow puts us to that inconvenience, it renders us on the other hand, a great service by facilitating the drawing from the forests of all the wood we have need of for buildings on land and vessels on the water, and for other purposes. We draw all this wood from the forests, by means of the sledges I have spoken of, with great ease, and much more conveniently and at much less cost than we could in summer by means of carts.

The air here is extremely healthy at all times ; but particularly in winter ; sickness is seldom seen in this country ; it is but little subject to drizzling rains or fogs ; the air here is extremely thin and keen. At the entrance to the gulf and river, drizzling rains are frequent, by reason of the proximity of the Ocean ; very few storms are seen here.

But how can we make money there? What can we get out of it all? This is a question that has often been put to me, and that gave me an inclination to laugh every time it was put to me ; I seemed to see people who wanted to reap a harvest before they had sowed any thing. After having said that the country is a good one, capable of producing all sorts of things, like France, that it is nealthy, that population only is wanting, that the country i- very extensive, and that without doubt there are great riches in it which we have not been able to bring to light, because we have an enemy who keeps us pent up in a little corner and prevents us from going about and making discoveries ; and so he will have to be destroyed, and many people will have to come into this country, and then we shall know the riches of it ; but some one will have to defray the cost of all this ; and who shall do it if not our good King? He has shown an inclination to do it, and may God be pleased to keep him still of the same mind.

Our neighbours, the English, laid out a great deal of money at the outset on the settlements they made ; they threw great numbers of people into them: so that now there are computed to be in them fifty thousand men capable of bearing arms ; it is a wonder to see their country now ; one finds all sorts of things there, the same as in Europe, and for half the price. They build numbers of ships, of all sorts and sizes ; they work iron mines ; they have beautiful cities ; they have stagecoaches and mails from one to the other; they have carriages like those in France ; those who laid out money there, are now getting good returns from it ; that country is not different from this ; what has been done there could be done here.

But all this shall not hinder me from telling you what I think could be done with great profit ; in the first place there is fishing for cod at the entrance of the gulf, and in the vicinity of Gaspé, where the fish abounds.

In the next place, there is oil to be got, from seals as well as from porpoises, of which there are plenty in the River Saint Lawrence, as I have said already. It is true that there would be some outlay to be made in this case, but it would not be great in comparison with the great profit that might be expected.

There are minerals, such as iron, copper, tin, lead and antimony to be mined for ; and many believe that there is also sulphur.

I have spoken to a manufacturer of salt petre, who tells me that it can be found here as good, and in as great quantity, as in any place in the world.

As for our charcoal from cedar wood, it is beyond comparison better than any other, for the manufacture of gunpowder and fire-works.

Besides, could not great profit be made out of the woods that are here in so great abundance, either by building ships with them or by using them for other works for which they are well adapted.

The soil being good, could not it be made to yield great profit, not only by means of all sorts of corn that could be grown in it, but also by means of hemp and flax, which grow so well here, that they could be cultivated on large scale with very great advantage ?

I say nothing about the numbers of animals that could be fed here, nor about many other things that you can see as well as I can after the descriptions I have given you.

Are all the rivers navigable? I answer yes, with the canoes of the Indians, but not with our vessels. Ships cannot pass Quebec, it is believed, and small vessels cannot go further than Montreal; between Montreal and the lake of the Iroquois, there are forty leagues of rapids which can only be ascended in canoes and flat-bottomed boats; and even these have to be towed, as boats are towed up the Seine All the great lakes beyond can be navigated in small vessels.

What hinders our rivers from being navigable is that falls or rapids are to be met with in them at intervals, and that in some more than in others; for in the River Saguenay one can go as far as from forty to fifty leagues in a large boat; while, on the contrary, in the river at Three-Rivers one cannot go more than four leagues in one; I have no doubt that if this country were settled several rivers that are not navigable might be made so, and that at a trifling cost; for instance there is a river in which there is only one rapid, a quarter of a league long, after which one might go a long way; yet, that one rapid makes it inaccessible to our boats.

It seems to me that I hear some one say: "you have told us much about the advantages of New France but you have not shown us its disadvantages, nor its inconveniences, yet we know well that there is not a country in the world however good it may be, in which something that is disagreeable is not met with." I answer that you are right It has been my study all along to make these things known to you; but in order to enable

you to understand them more clearly, I shall here specify
in detail what I consider the most troublesome and disagreeable things, and these I shall include under four
heads.

The first is that our enemies, the Iroquois keep us so
closely pent up that they hinder us from enjoying the
advantages of the country. We cannot go to hunt or fish
without danger of being killed or taken prisoners by those
rascals; and we cannot even plough out fields, much less
make hay, without continual risk :) They lie in ambush
on all sides, and any little thicket suffices for six or
seven of those barbarians to put themselves under cover
in, or more correctly speaking in an ambush, from which
they throw themselves upon you suddenly when you are
at your work, or going to it or coming from it. They
never attack but when they are the strongest; if they are
the weakest they do not say a word; if by accident they
are discoveved they fly, leaving every thing behind
them ; and as they are fleet of foot it is difficult to catch
them ; so you see we are always in dread, and a poor
fellow does not work in safety if he has to go ever so
little a way off to his work. Wives are always uneasy
lest their husbands, who have gone away to their work
in the morning, should be killed or taken prisoners and
they should never see them again ; and these Indians are
the cause of the greater number of our settlers being
poor, not only through our not being able to enjoy the
advantages of the country as I have just said, but
because they often kill cattle, sometimes hinder the gathe-
ring in of the harvest, and at other times burn and
plunder houses when they can take people by surprise.
This is a great evil, but it is not beyond remedy, and we
expect one from the benevolence of our good King, who

has told me that he wishes to deliver us from it. It would not be very difficult to do so, for there are not among them more than eight hundred or nine hundred men capable of bearing arms. It is true they are war-like men, and very dexterous at fighting in the woods; they have given proof of this to our Commanders from France who despised them; some of these were killed and others were forced to admit that one must not neglect to take precautions when one goes to war with them, that they understand the business, and that on this score they are not barbarians; but after all, a thousand or twelve hundred men well led would give occasion for its being said " they were but they are not ;" and to have exterminated a tribe that has caused so many others to perish and is the terror of all these countries, would raise the reputation of the French very high throughout New France.

The second inconvenience I find here arises from the mosquitoes, otherwise called gnats, which abound greatly in the forests during three months of summer; there are but few of them in the open country, because they cannot stand the wind, the least breath of which blows them away; but in the woods, where they are sheltered from the wind they are very troublesome, more particularly in the mornings and evenings, and they sting more sharply when it is going to rain than at any other time. Some persons have had their faces very much swollen from their bites; but this does not last, and at the end of twenty-four hours it hardly shows at all; smoke drives them away, and for that reason one always lights a fire and makes a smoke near one when one sleeps in a wood.

The third in convenience I find arises from the length of the winter, especially about Quebec. I will not say any more about this, as I have already said enough of it above; I will only say that the snow is from three to four feet deep there, I mean at Quebec. for in the other settlements there is much less, as I have already said.

In the Iroquois country, there are snakes called rattle snakes whose bite is dangerous; I have spoken of them already, therefore I shall not say any thing more about them, except that there are not any of them in these parts.   These are the greatest inconveniences I know of.

Here is another set of questions that have been put to me, namely : how we live in this country. whether justice is administered, if there is not great debauchery, seeing that numbers of worthless fellows and bad girls come here, it is said.

I will answer all these questions one after the other, beginning with the last.   It is not true that those sort of girls come hither, and those who say so have made a great mistake, and have taken the Islands of Saint Christophe and Martinique for New France ; if any of them come here, they are not known for such ; for before any can be taken on board ship to come here some of their relations or friends must certify that they have always been well-behaved; if by chance there are found among those who have, some who are in disrepute, or who are said to have misconducted themselves on the voyage out, they are sent back to France.

As for the scapegraces, if any come over it is only because they are not known for what they are, and when they are in the country they have to live like decent people, otherwise they would have a bad time of it ; we know how to hang people in this country as well as they do elsewhere, and we have proved it to some who have not been well behaved.

Justice is administered here, and there are Judges; and those who are not satisfied with their decisions can appeal to the Governor and the Sovereign Council, appointed by the King, and sitting at Quebec.

Hitherto we have lived pleasantly enough, for it has pleased God to give us Governors who have all been good men, and besides we have had the Jesuit Fathers who take great pains to teach the people what is right so that all goes on peaceably; we live much in the fear of God. and nothing scandalous takes place without its being put to rights immediately; there is great religious devotion throughout the country.

CHAPTER XIV.

CONTINUATION OF THE SAME SUBJECT.

Several persons after having heard me speak of New France, whether they felt inclined to come to it or not, have put these questions to me: "Do you think I would be fit for that country? What would have to be done in order to get there? If I took four or five thousand francs with me, could I with such a sum make myself tolerably comfortable?" And after these several other questions which I shall mention after having answered these.

(You ask me in the first place whether you are fit for this country. The answer I make you is that this country is not yet fit for people of rank who are extremely rich. because such people would not find in it all the luxuries they enjoy in France; such persons must wait until this country has more inhabitants, unless they are persons who wish to retire from the world in order to lead a pleasant and quiet life free from fuss, or who are inclined to immortalize themselves by building cities or by other great works in this new world

The people best fitted for this country are those who can work with their own hands in making clearings, putting up buildings and otherwise; for as men's wages are very high here, a man who does not take care and practice economy will be ruined; but the best way is always to begin by clearing land and making a good farm, and to attend to other things only after that has been done, and not to do like some whom I have seen, who paid out all their money for the erection of fine buildings which they had to sell afterwards for less than the cost.

I am supposing myself to be speaking to persons who would come to settle in this country with a view to making a living out of it, and not to trade.

It would be well for a man coming to settle, to bring provisions with him for at least a year or two years if possible, especially flour which he could get for much less in France and could not even be sure of being always able to get for any money here; for if many people should come from France in any year without bringing any flour with them and the grain crops should be bad here that year, which God forbid, they would find themselves much straitened.

It would be well also to bring a supply of clothes, for they cost twice as much here as they do in France.

Money is also much dearer; its value increases one third, so that a coin of fifteen *sous* is worth twenty, and so on in proportion.

I would advise a man having money enough to bring

two labouring men with him, or even more if he has the means, to clear his land ; this is in answer to the question whether a person having three thousand or four thousand francs to employ here could do so with advantage ; such a person could get himself into very easy circumstances in three or four years if he choose to practice economy, as I have already said.

Most of our settlers are persons who came over in the capacity of servants, and who, after serving their masters for three years, set up for themselves. They had not worked for more than a year before they had cleared land on which they got in more than enough grain for their food. They have but little, generally when they set up for themselves, and marry wives who are no better off than they are ; yet. if they are fairly hard working people you see them in four or five years in easy circumstances and well fitted out for persons of their condition in life.

Poor people would be much better off here than they are in France, provided they are not lazy : they could not fail to get, employment and could not say, as they do in France, that they are obliged to beg for their living because they cannot find any one to give them work ; in one word, no people are wanted, either men or women, who cannot turn their hands to some work, unless they are very rich.

Women's work consists of household work and of feeding and caring for the cattle ; for there are few female servants ; so that wives are obliged to do their own house work ; nevertheless those who have the means employ valets who do the work of maidservants.

11

CHAPTER XV.

As I have still a little time left I will make up another chapter of several things I have omitted in the preceding ones, which will not be disagreeable to the curious reader.

I have already spoken of a spring in the Iroquois country, the water of which the Iroquois use in the place of oil. When this is stirred with a stick as it were flames are thrown out; but, as I have already said, this water is not good either to burn or to drink, but only for greasing things with.

That lead mine I have spoken of, which is not very far from where I am writing, yields from sixty to seventy per cent, and the Iroquois hew out with their axes long narrow splinters of the rock which they cut across into small pieces for use when they fall short of bullets in time of war.

In Lake Superior, there is a large island, of about fifty leagues in circumference, on which there is a very rich bed of copper ore. Large lumps of pure copper are to be found there in several places.

There are other places in that neighbourhood where there are similar beds, as I have learned from four or five Frenchmen, lately returned from thence, who had gone thither in company with a Jesuit Father, sent there on a mission, who has since died. They passed three years there before they could find an opportunity to get away; they told me that they had seen a nugget of pure copper, on the side of a hill, that would weigh more than eight hundred pounds, according to their estimate; they say that the Indians when they pass that way. make fires on top of it and then hew pieces out of it with their axes, and that one of themselves broke his axe in the act of trying to do the same; it would not be difficult to get there if we were masters of the Iroquois and could go through their great lake.

They informed me also that beautiful blue stones, believed to be turquoises, are also to be found there.

Green stones like emeralds, are found there also.

There are diamonds there also, but I do not know if they are pure ones or not. They were not able to go to the place where these stones are, because the Indians were not willing to guide them to it without being paid for doing so, seeing that it was pretty far off, and they being poor, did not dare to risk the expense, not being sufficiently well informed on the subject to be able to judge whether the stones were valuable or not.

Red stones, of two shades of colour, are found there also, some being scarlet and others of the colour of the blood of an ox; the Indians make *calumets* or pipes of them, for smoking tobacco, which they think a great deal of.

There are dyes also, of all sorts of colours, that the Indians make use of, of which I shall not give you any description, because I do not know them well, with the exception of the root of a tree which they use for dying things of flame colour, and which is of a very vivid hue. For dyeing other colours they make use of plants, stones and earths. All I can say is that most of the colours they use seem to me to be very bright and beautiful. I have seen in use among them a blue, like our azure, and I do not know that it is not the same.

In the Iroquois country, that is to say, where the Onontagués live, there is white chalk which the Dutch have sometimes gone there to fetch some of, telling the Indians it was for the purpose of whitening their linen.

Near Lake Saint Francis, which is about fourteen or fifteen leagues above Montreal, there is one of the finest groves of oak in the world, as well for the beauty of the trees in it as for its extent; it is more than twenty leagues long, and no one knows how wide.

THE END.

CONTENTS:

www.ingramcontent.com/pod-product-compliance
Lightning Source LLC
Chambersburg PA
CBHW020307090426
42735CB00009B/1257